I0462474

THIS BOOK

BELONGS TO

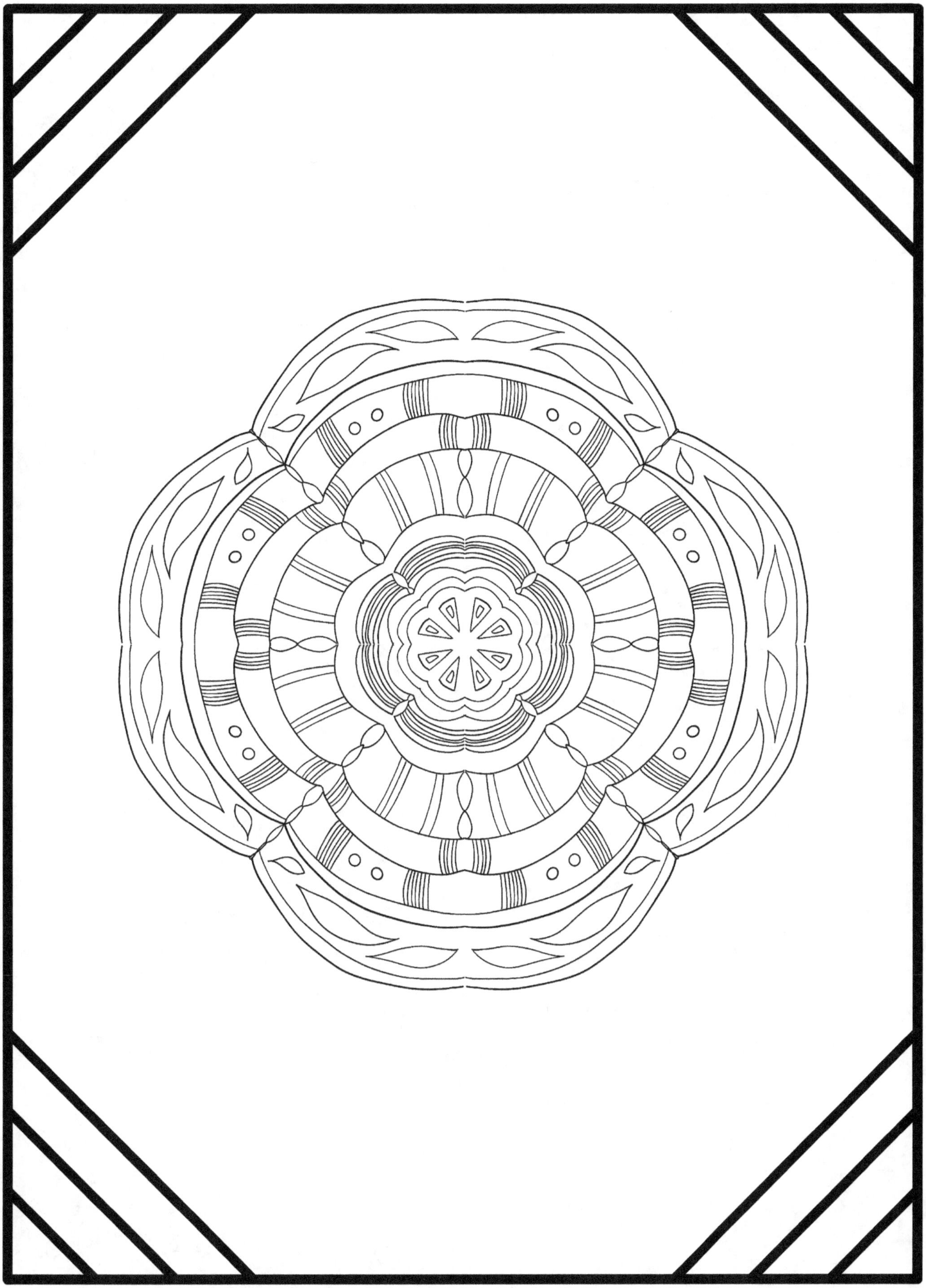

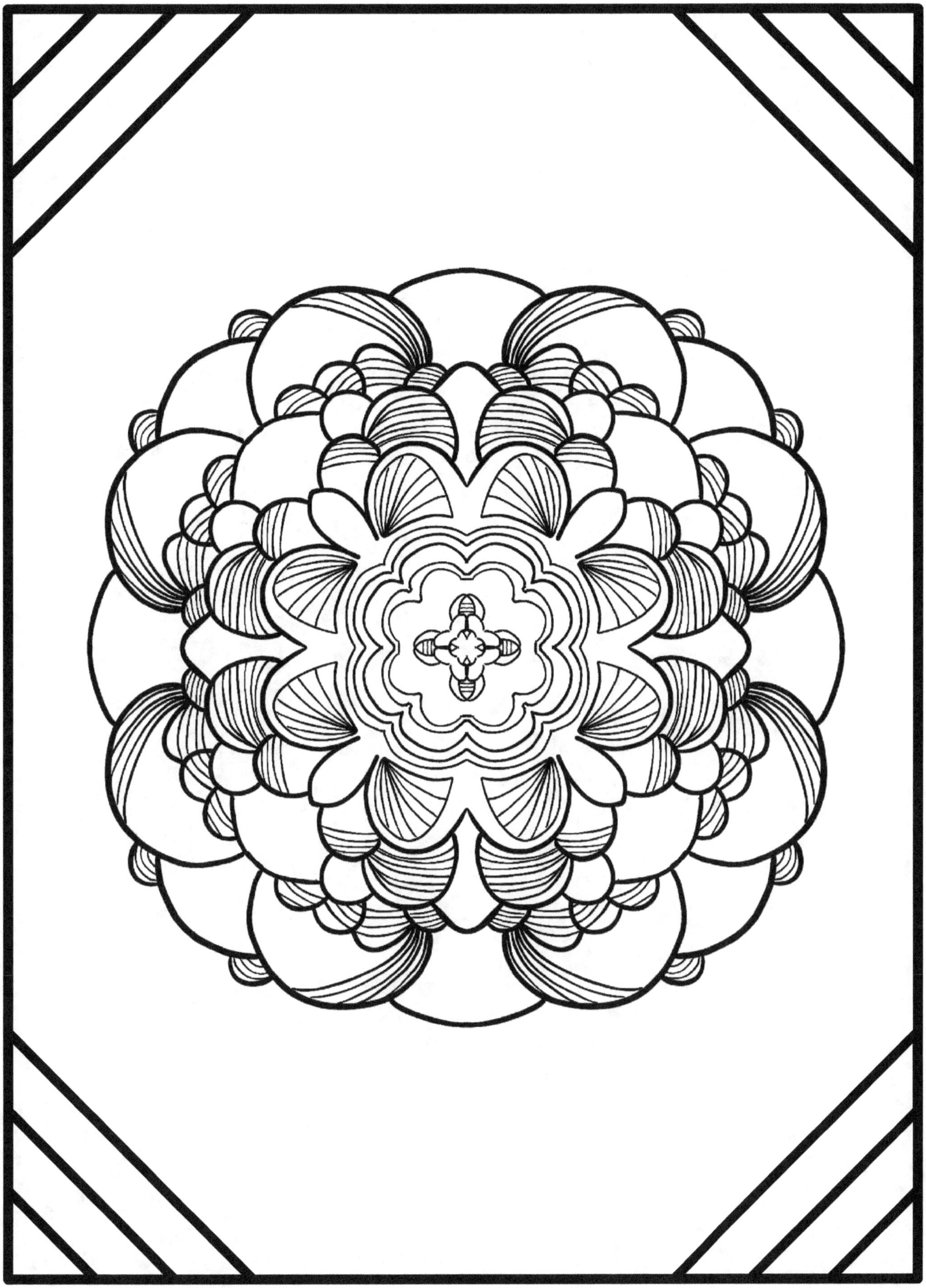

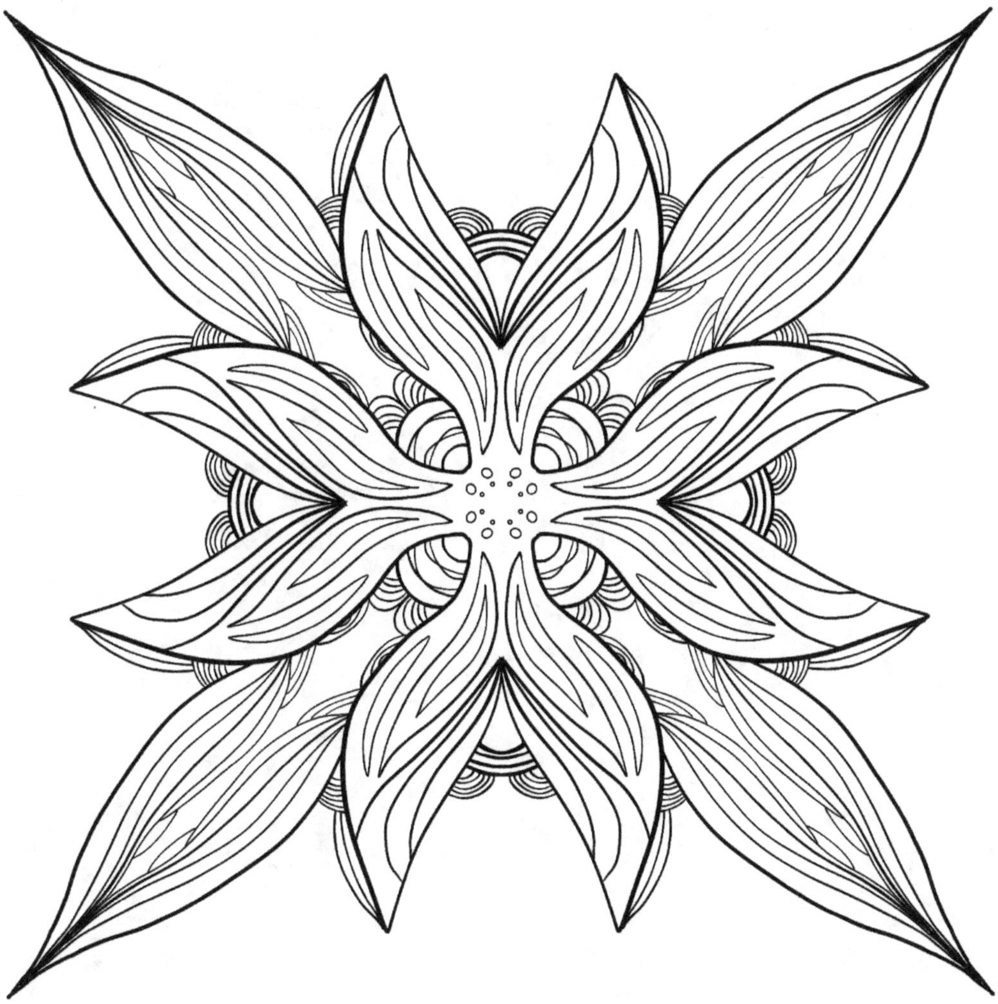

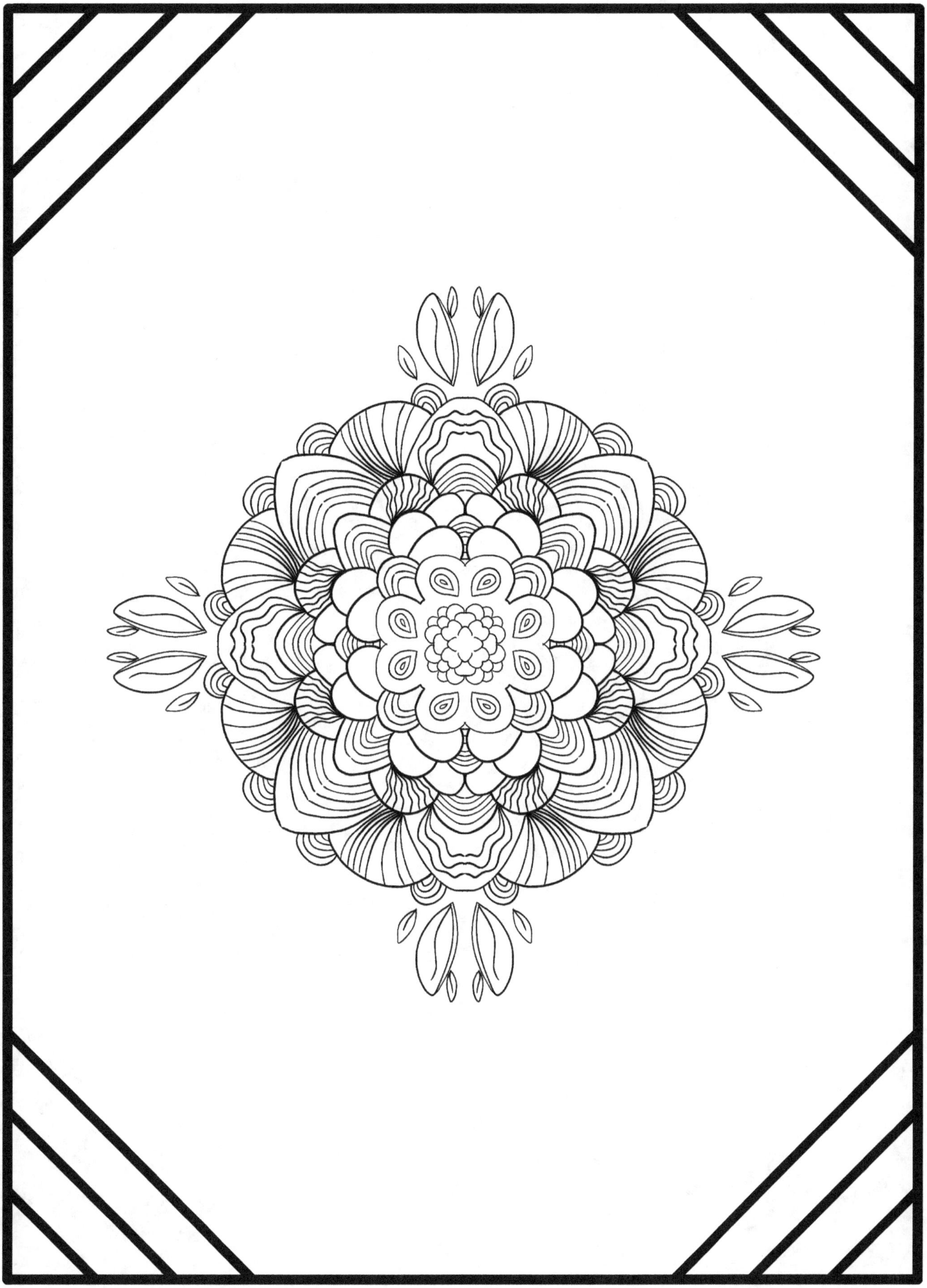

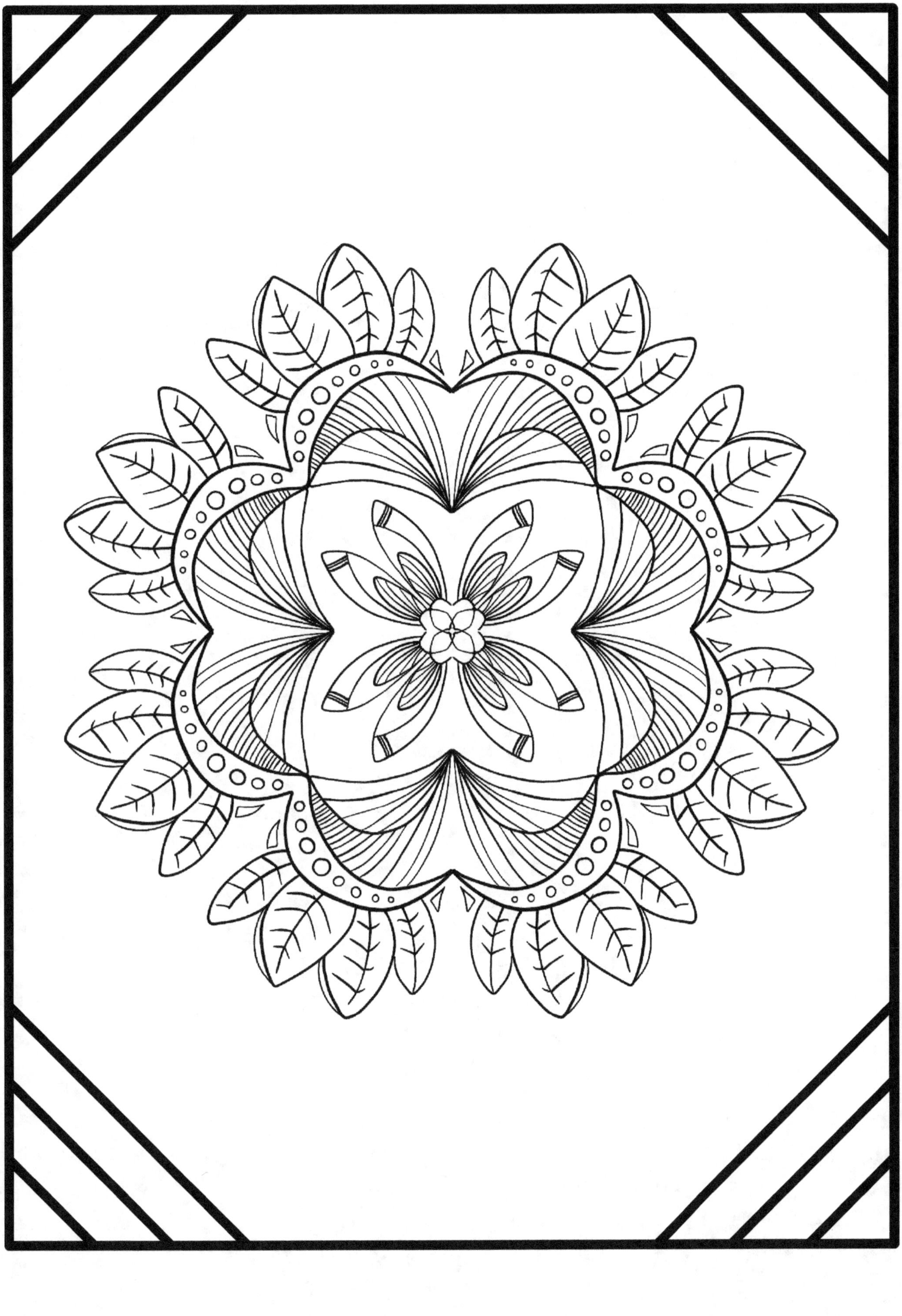

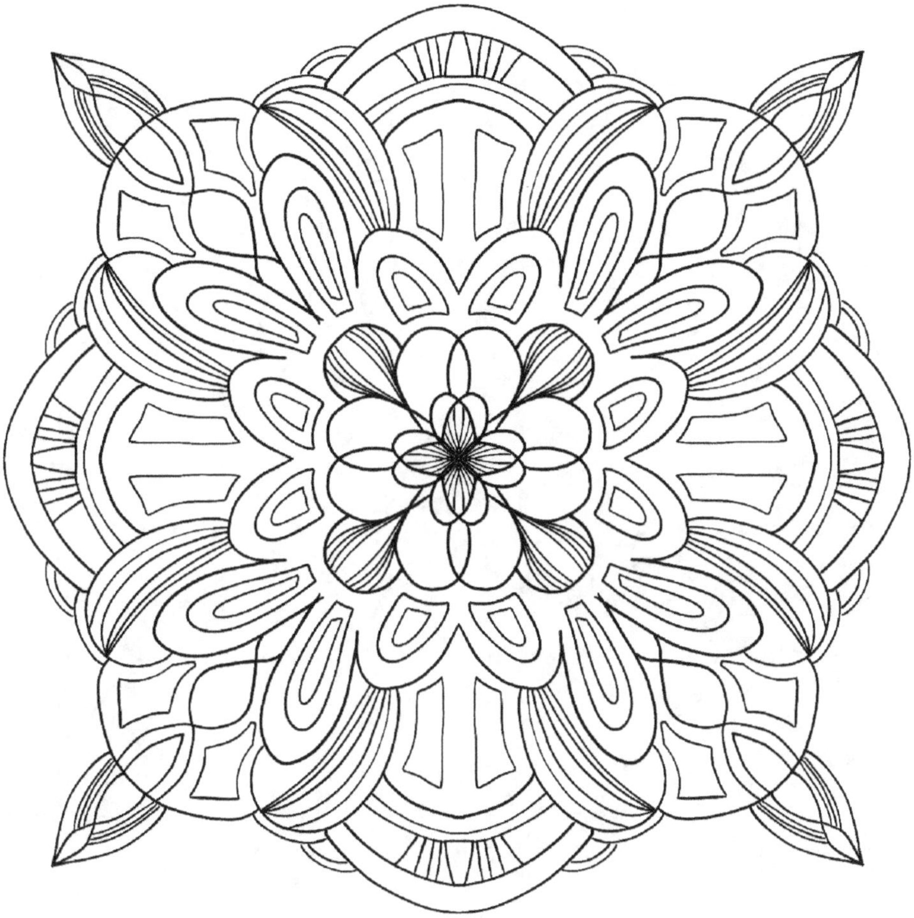

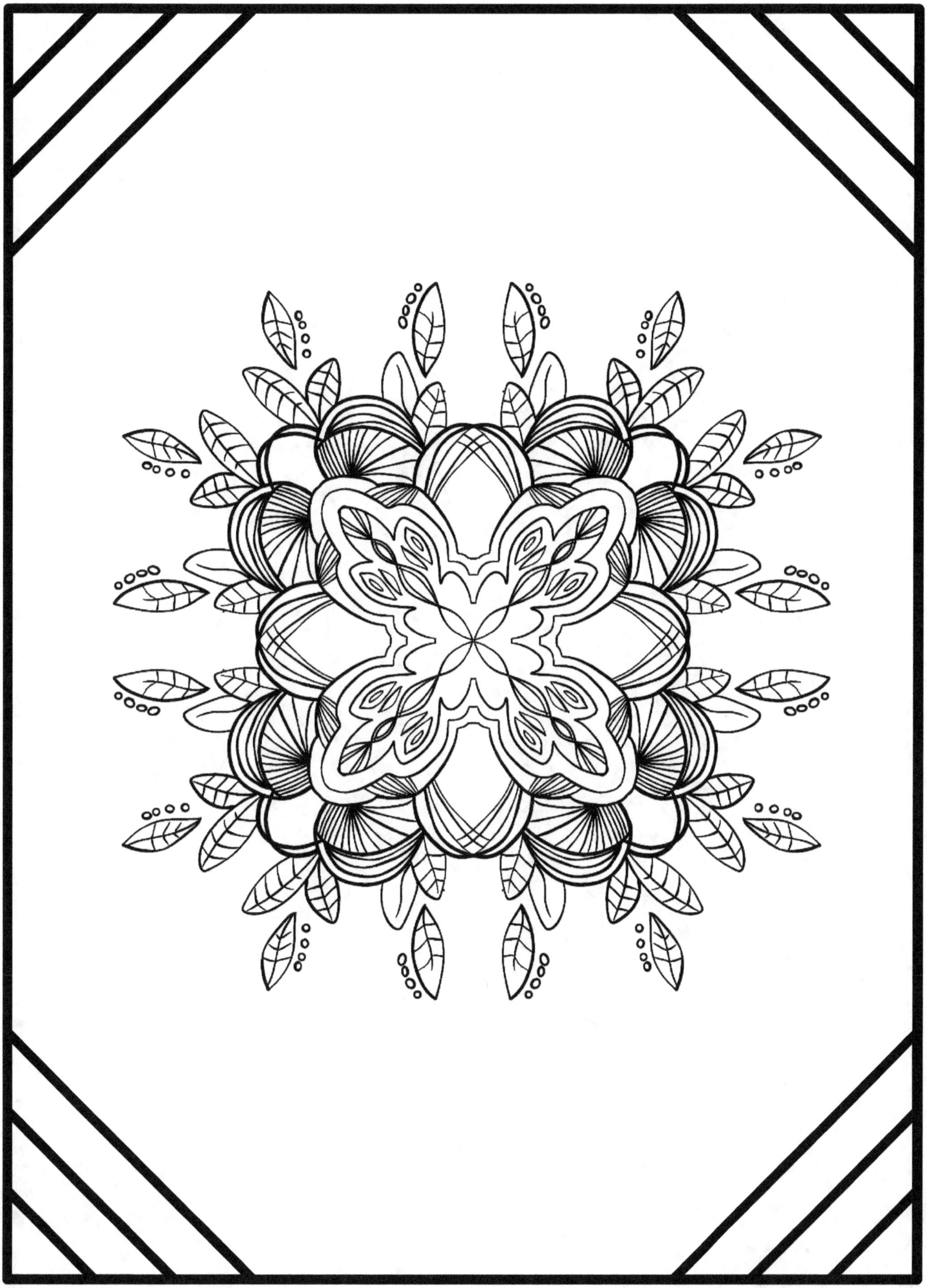

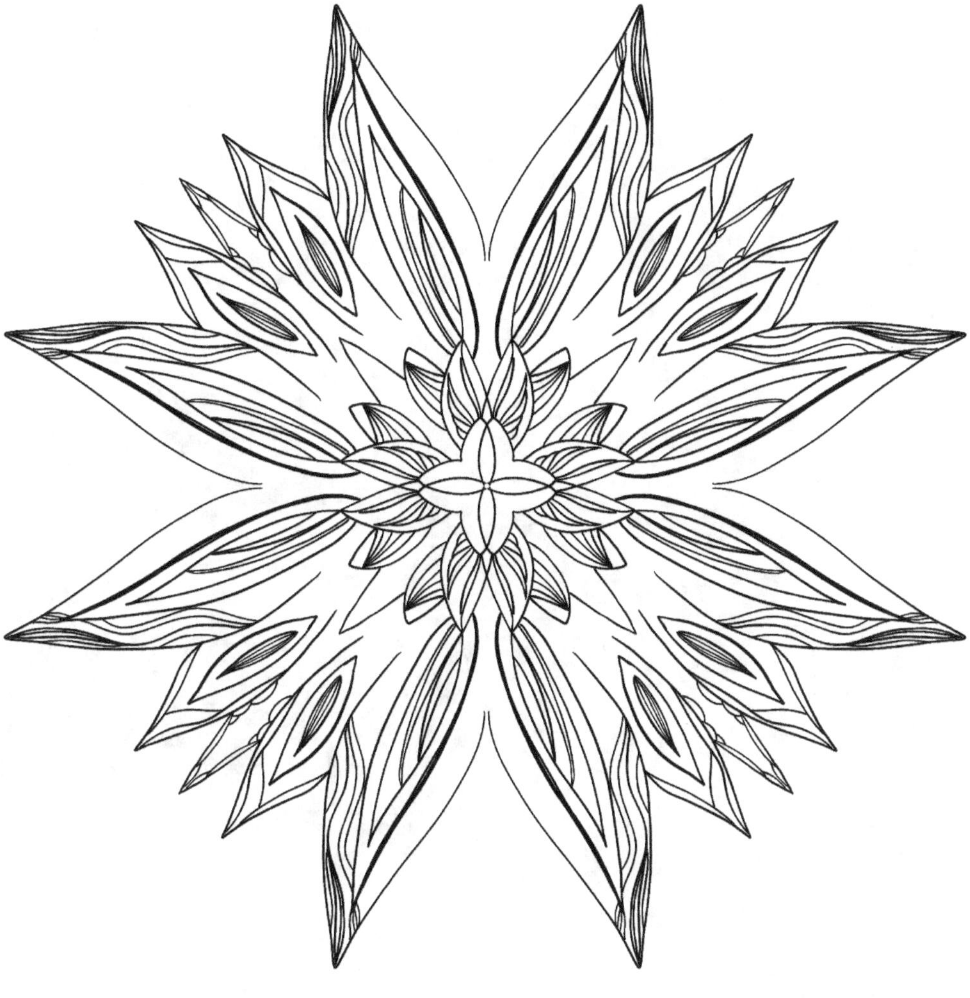

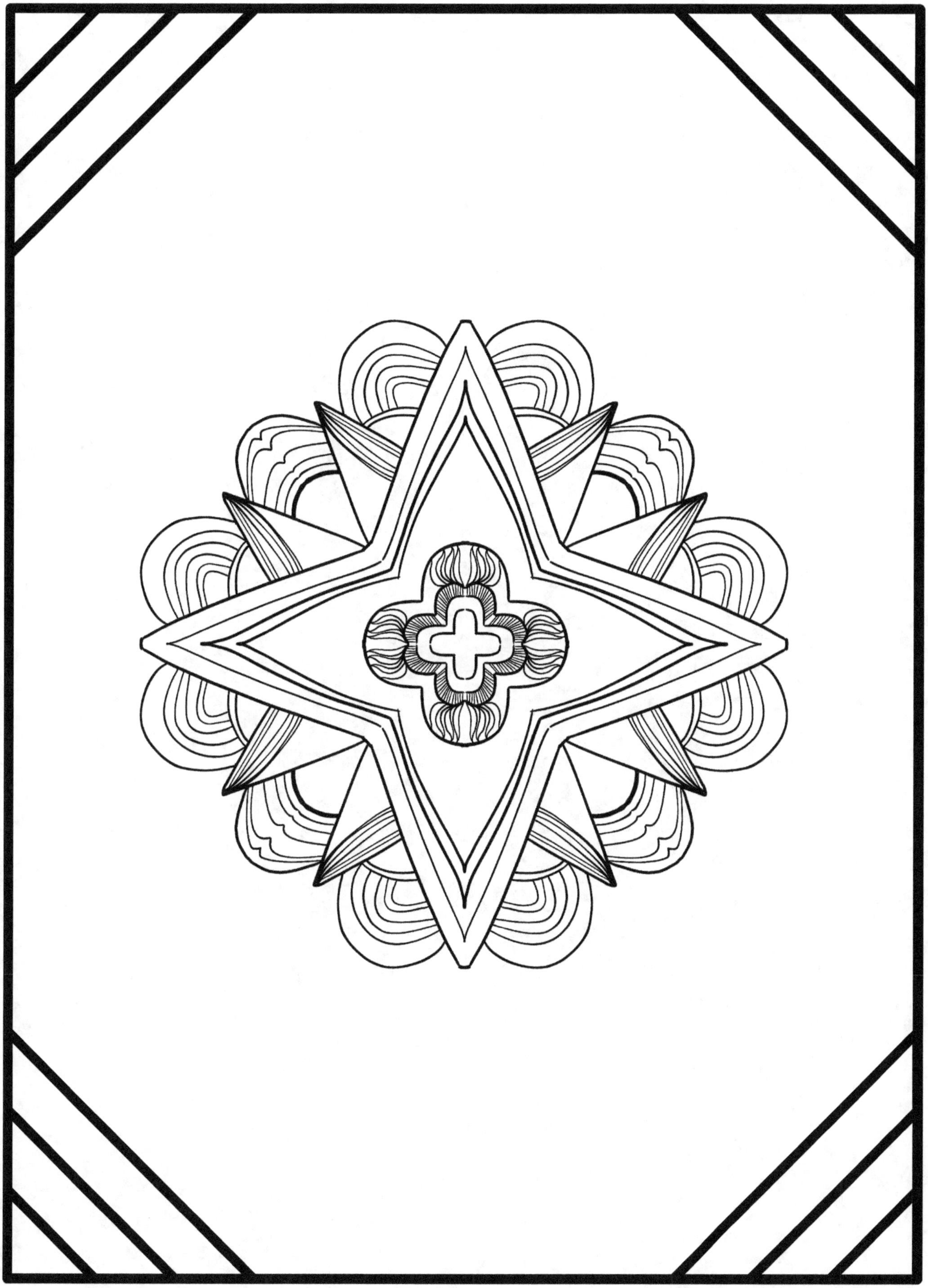

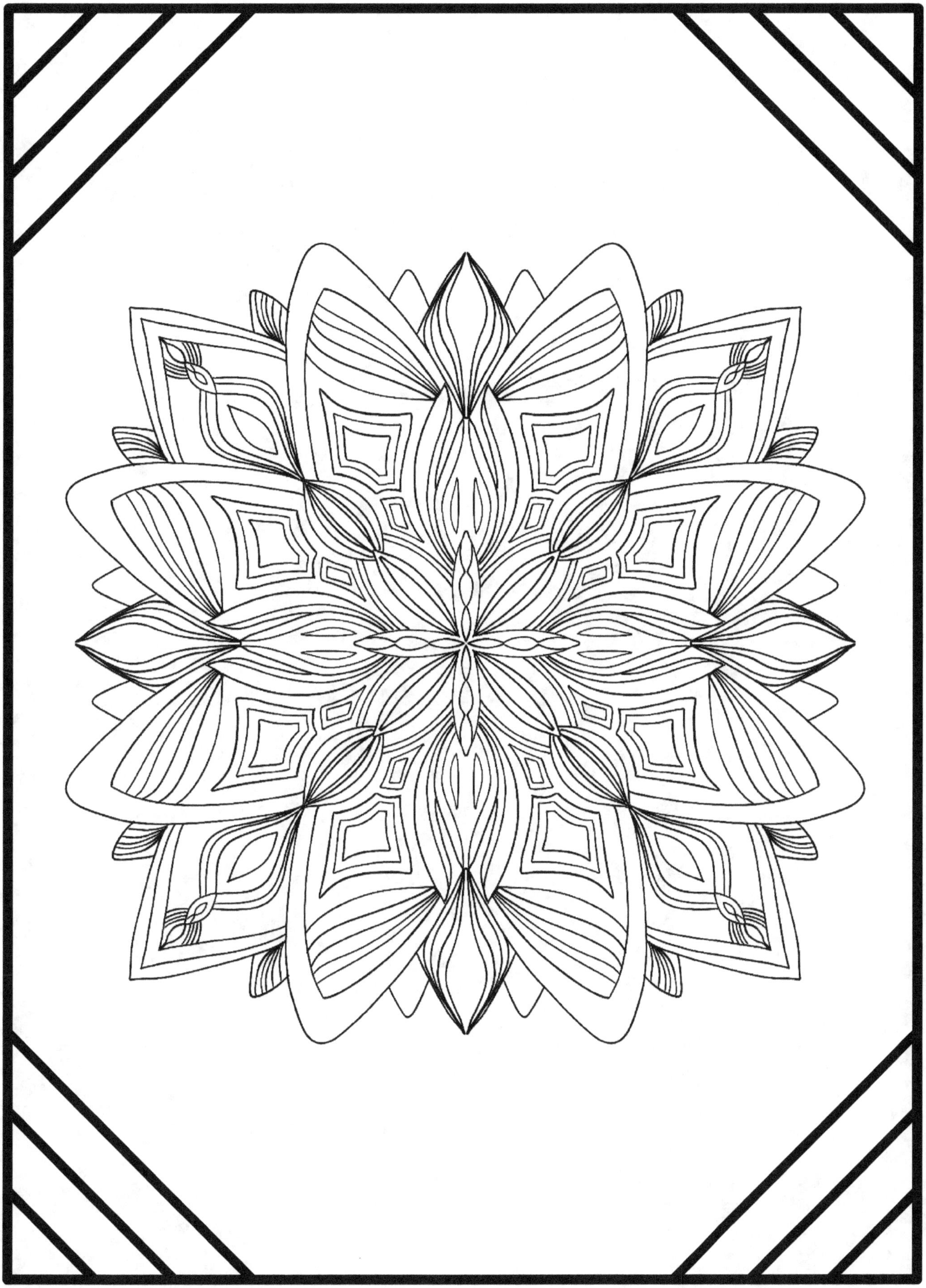

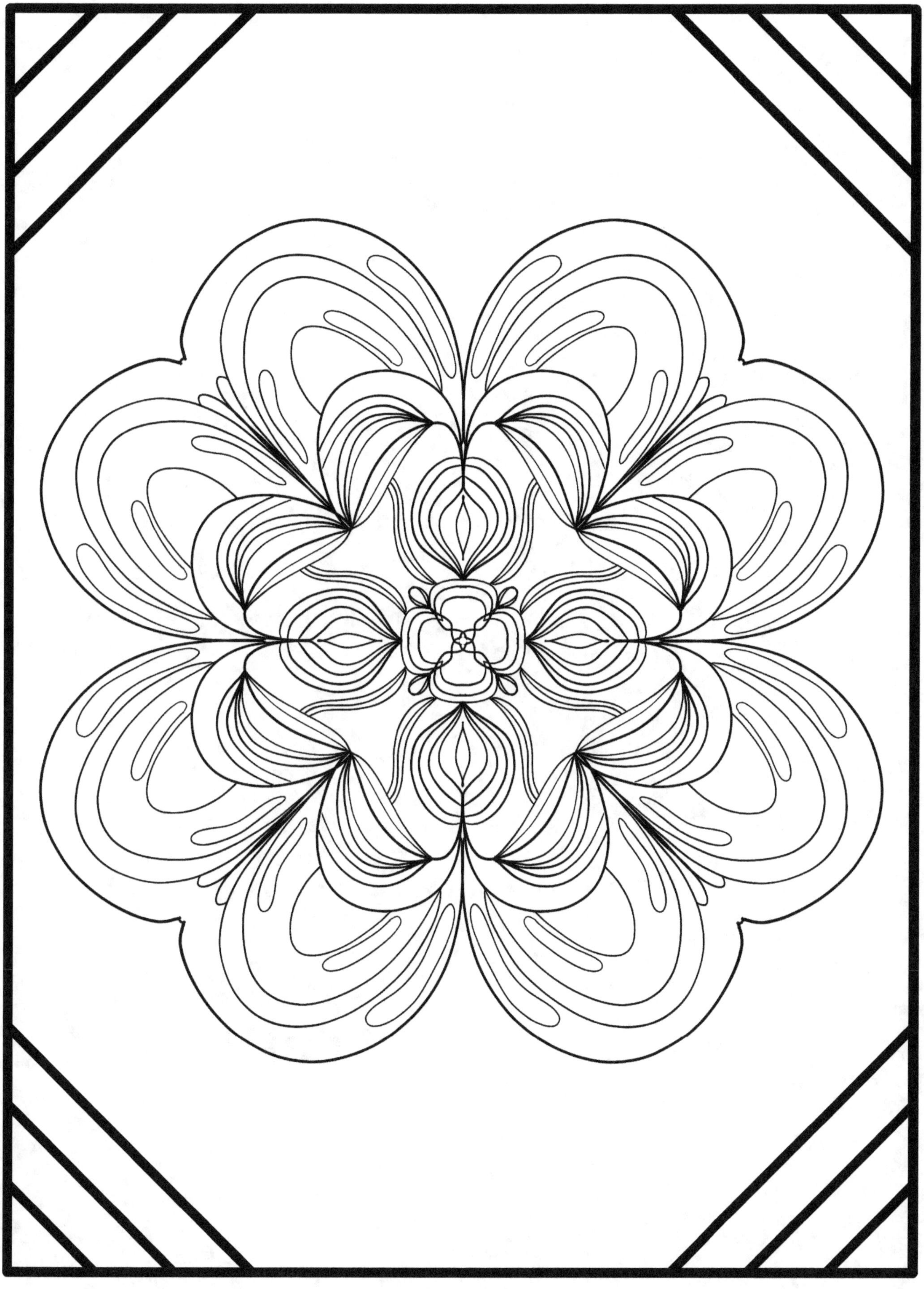

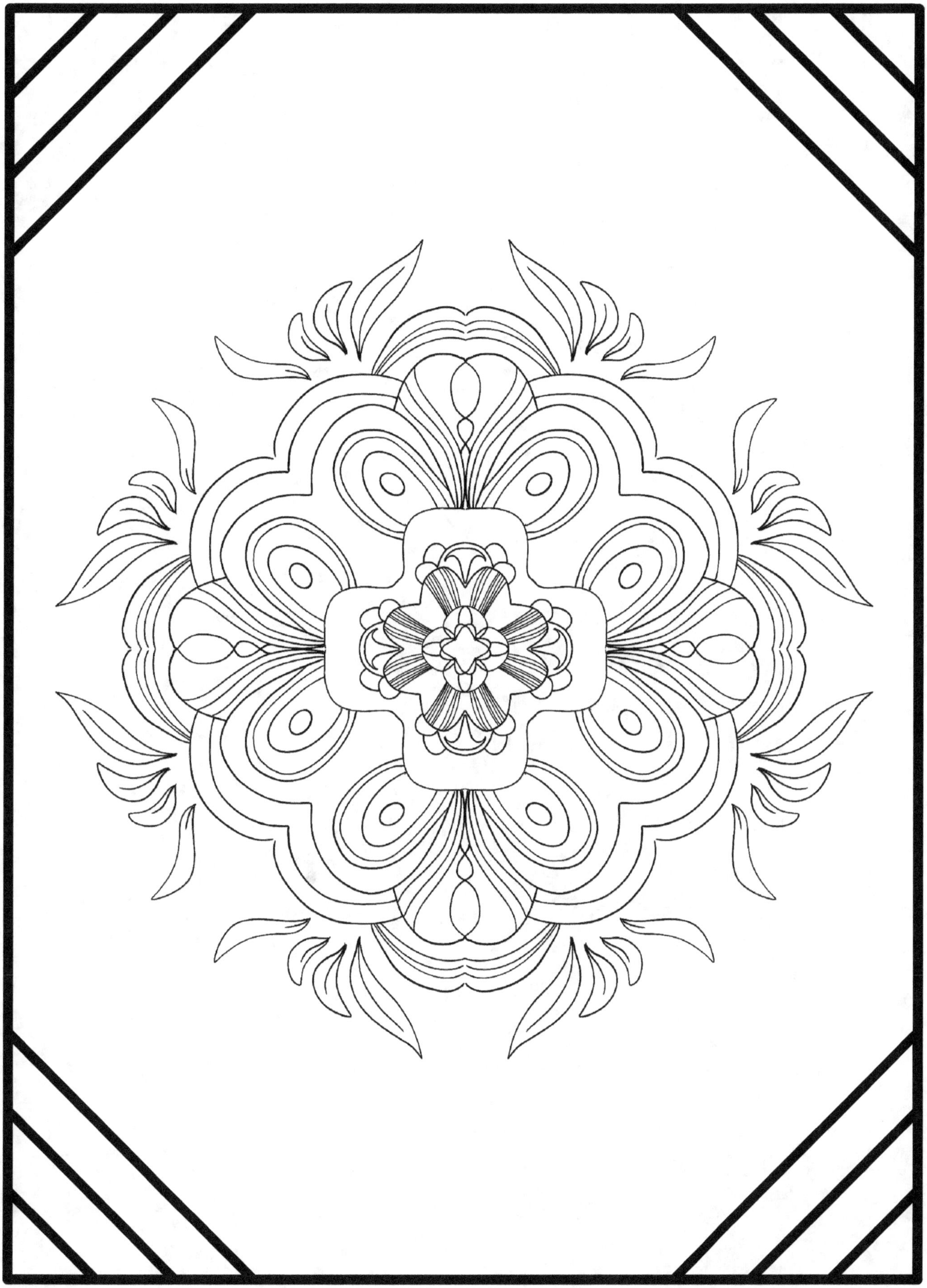

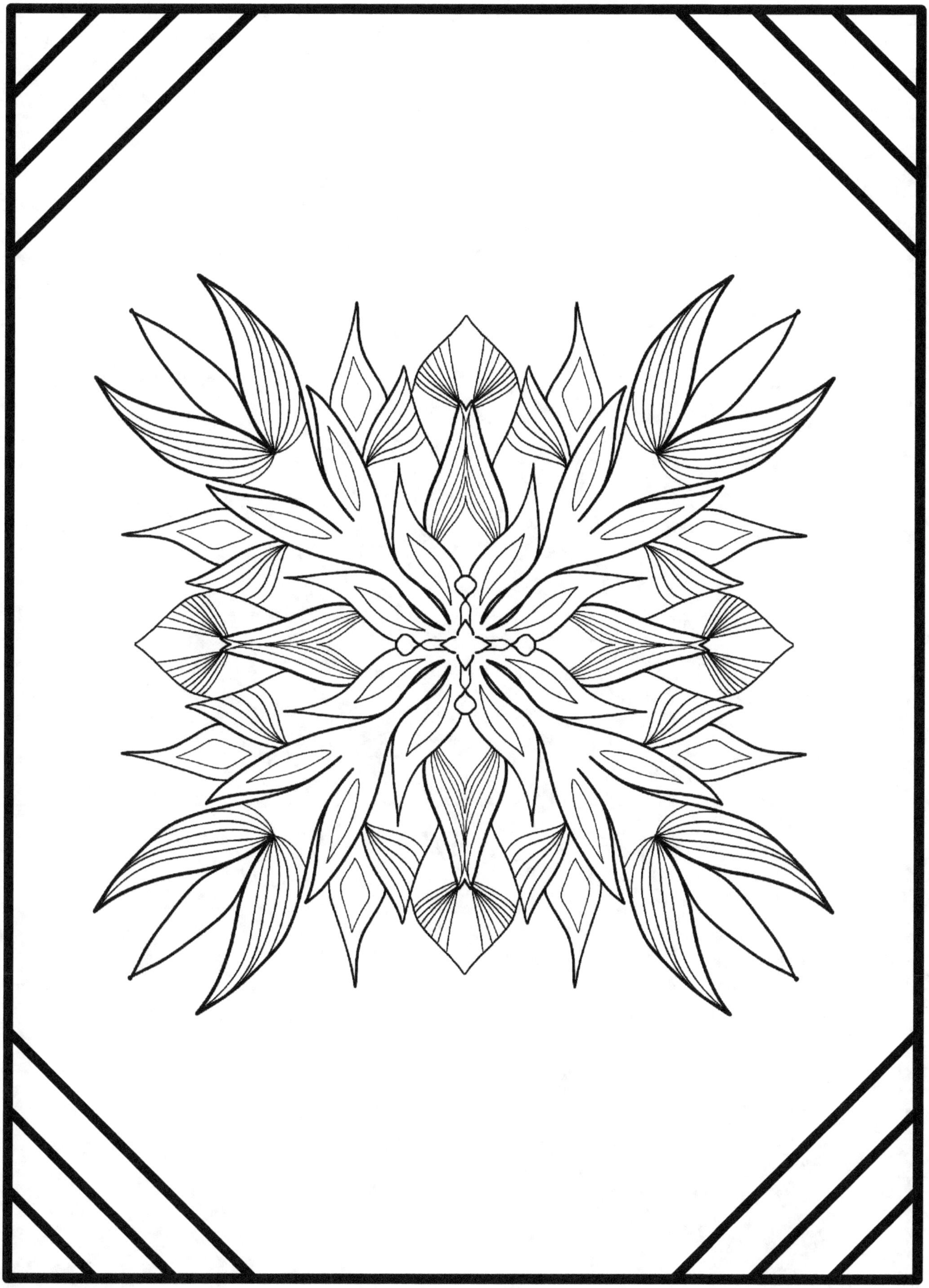

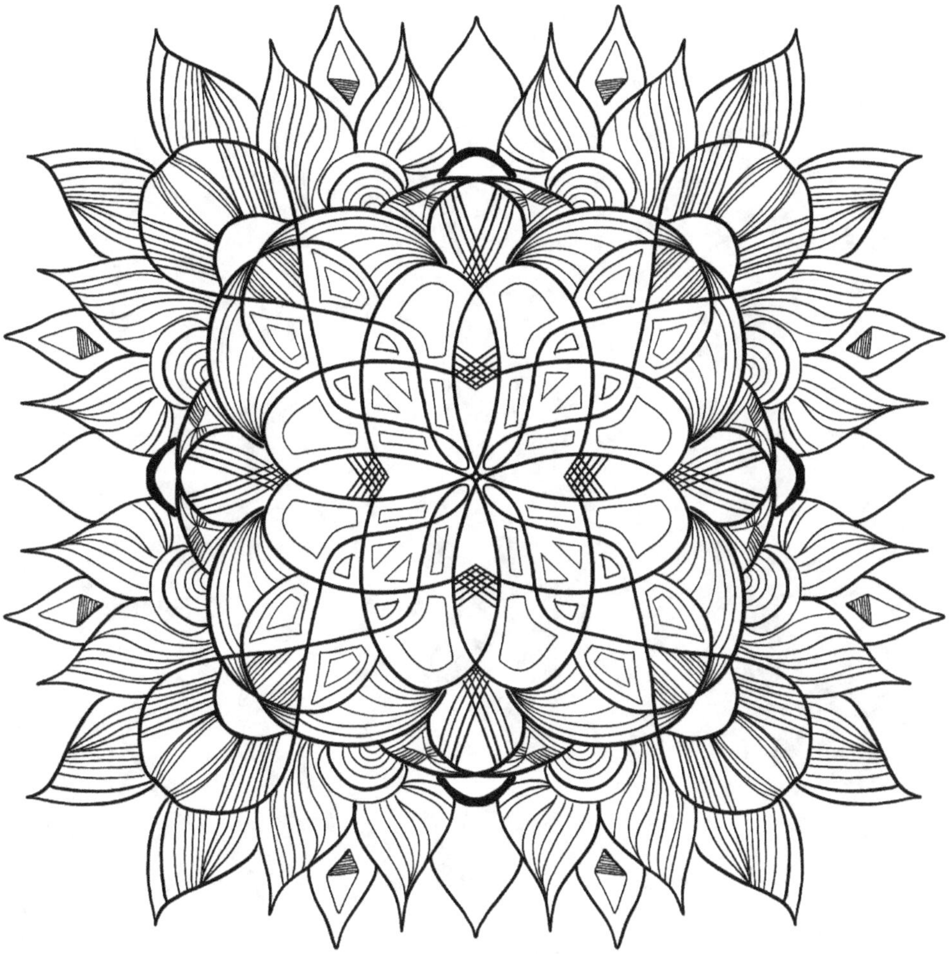

www.ingramcontent.com/pod-product-compliance
Lightning Source LLC
Chambersburg PA
CBHW081148170526
45158CB00009BA/2773
* 9 7 8 1 0 8 7 0 0 8 2 8 8 *